Practical Design & Technology

Mechanical Constructions

Steven Atkin & Richard Beeden

www.heinemann.co.uk/library

Visit our website to find out more information about **Heinemann Library** books.

To order:
☎ Phone 44 (0) 1865 888066
📄 Send a fax to 44 (0) 1865 314091
💻 Visit the Heinemann Bookshop at www.heinemann.co.uk/library to browse our catalogue and order online.

First published in Great Britain by Heinemann Library, Halley Court, Jordan Hill, Oxford OX2 8EJ, part of Harcourt Education.
Heinemann is a registered trademark of Harcourt Education Ltd.

Editorial: Andrew Farrow, Lucy Thunder and Helen Cox
Design: David Poole and Paul Myerscough
Illustrations: Geoff Ward and Darren Lingard
Picture Research: Catherine Bevan and Rebecca Sodergren
Production: Séverine Ribierre

Originated by Ambassador Litho Ltd
Printed in China by W K T Co.Ltd

ISBN 0 431 17581 0 (hardback)
07 06 05 04 03
10 9 8 7 6 5 4 3 2 1

ISBN 0 431 17585 3 (paperback)
08 07 06 05 04
10 9 8 7 6 5 4 3 2 1

British Library Cataloguing in Publication Data

Atkin, Steven and Beeden, Richard
Mechanical constructions. - (Practical design & technology)
621
A full catalogue record for this book is available from the British Library.

Acknowledgements

The publishers would like to thank the following for permission to reproduce photographs:
Alamy Images p5b; Gareth Boden pp**7**, **14a**, **14b**, **14c**, **15a**, **15b**, 20, **22a**, **26a**, **26b**, **29a**, **29b**, **29c**, **29d**, **31a**, **32b**, **36a**, **36b**, **39a**, **39b**, **39c**, **39d**, **40a**, **40b**, **42a**, **42b**, **43a**, **43b**, **43c**; Bridgeman Art Library p**10**; Cabaret Mechanical Theatre (Heini Schneebeli) pp**24**, **25**; Peter Evans p**4c**; National Maritime Museum p**4b**; Photodisc p**8**; Tudor Photography pp**5a**, **12**, **13**, **16**, **30**, **31**, **32a**, **33**, **34**, **35a**, **35b**, **35c**, **40**.

Cover photograph of the the barking dog project and the mechanical spider project, reproduced with permission of Gareth Boden.

The publishers would like to thank Andy Bird for his assistance in the preparation of this book and the staff and pupils of both Hope Valley College, Derbyshire and Wales High School, Rotherham. Thanks also to Cabaret Mechanical Theatre.

Every effort has been made to contact copyright holders of any material reproduced in this book. Any omissions will be rectified in subsequent printings if notice is given to the publishers.

Contents

Any words appearing in the text in bold, **like this,** are explained in the Glossary.

Introduction to mechanics

Mechanics is one of the most fascinating and important fields of technology. This book provides an interesting introduction to the world of mechanical engineering.

The book looks at **mechanism** projects that you could design and make either at school or at home. The projects are broken down into small stages so you can follow them easily. It explains the different stages of design technology project work that are needed for the design and manufacturing process, such as product **analysis**, design **specifications** and product **evaluation**.

What are mechanisms?

Mechanisms are a part of our daily lives – we all use them. Mechanisms are usually made of moving parts. Simple items such as door handles and locks contain mechanisms. Many more complex products, like cars, bicycles, sewing machines and pushchairs, all need and use different types of mechanisms in order to work properly.

Why do we use mechanisms?

We use mechanisms because they help us to complete a job or task more easily. For example, a screwdriver is a simple mechanism. Imagine trying to undo a tight screw without one! The screwdriver mechanism applies **torque**, which makes it much easier to tighten or release a screw.

What do mechanisms do?

Mechanisms can do a number of different jobs. Their two main functions are:

- to change one type of motion into a different type of motion
- to **transmit** speed, movement and force.

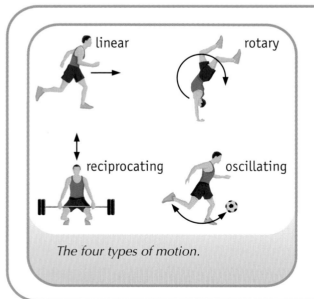

The four types of motion.

What is motion?

Motion is a direction of movement. There are four different types of motion:

1. **Linear** motion – this movement is forward in a straight line, for example the way a train moves.

2. **Rotary** motion – turning and spinning around, like a child's roundabout, for example.

3. **Reciprocating** motion – motion back and forth in a straight line, like a **piston**.

4. **Oscillating** motion – swinging motion, back and forth in an arc, like a **pendulum**.

What is a mechanical system?

A **mechanical system** is a simple way of showing what a mechanism will do. It is made up of three parts: the input, process and **output**.

Input, process and output

The input is usually a type of force or motion. This is converted by a mechanism, the process, into an output motion or force. The output motion is generally different from the input motion.

Locking a door involves rotary input (turning the key) and linear output (the bolt sliding into the door frame).

This canal mechanism called the Falkirk Wheel, near Falkirk, is an example of oscillating motion.

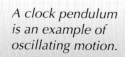

A clock pendulum is an example of oscillating motion.

The Millennium Eye in London is an example of rotary motion.

The design process

The task of designing and making something is very complicated. The designer needs to think about a wide range of different things, from the materials that could be used to the requirements of the **consumer**. The whole activity is often described as the 'design process'. The design process is a framework for designing and making and is used by designers all over the world in the design and manufacture of a wide range of products. This book will explore the design process for designing and making mechanical products – that is, products that are designed and manufactured using **mechanisms**. The design process has nine stages and is as follows:

Stage 1

Identifying an area of need or opportunity – this is where a company, designer or individual identifies a problem with an existing product, or sees an opportunity to develop a new product.

Stage 2

Developing a **design brief** – this is a statement that describes the problem that needs to be solved.

Stage 3

Research – this stage involves finding out as much information about the design brief as possible. There are many different areas of research, but the main ones are:

- Product **analysis** – looking at existing products and thinking about how they can help in the design of a product.
- Users – finding out what people (consumers) want from the product.
- Materials and **components** – finding out what materials could be used to make the product and what components could be utilized in the design.
- Equipment – finding out about the different machines and processes that could be used in manufacturing the product.

Stage 4

Design **specification** – this is the development of a precise description of what the product must have and do.

Stage 5

Design ideas – this is the generation of a number of ideas that meet the requirements of the design specification. They are usually sketched by hand initially, but they can also be developed using Computer Aided Design (CAD) programs such as Adobe Illustrator®.

Stage 6

Product development – this is the process of getting from a number of design ideas to being ready to manufacture the first version of the product (the **prototype**). This stage involves **modelling** different ways of making the product, and the production of working drawings and manufacturing instructions.

Stage 7

Planning – this is working out how to make the final product. This stage involves making an action plan. Sometimes this is also shown in the form of a **flowchart**, with different symbols used to represent different stages of the manufacturing process.

Stage 8

Manufacturing – this is the making of your product.

Stage 9

Testing and evaluation – it is very important that the product is fully tested to check that it meets the requirements of the design specification. **Evaluating** means thinking about how well the project has gone. It can be broken down into three main questions:

1 What have I done well?
2 What could I have done better?
3 How could I improve the finished product?

! Health and safety

General

- Care should be taken when using craft knives or sharp cutting tools. Always make sure knife blades and scissor blades are held correctly and carried with care.
- Tie back long hair.
- Remove jewellery such as long earrings.
- Wear sensible footwear.

Eye protection

During making operations, using tools such as drills and lathes and so on, eye protection should be worn. Protective goggles or spectacles should be approved to **British Standard** (BS) 2092 or equivalent.

Cutting mats

Always use a suitable cutting mat to protect work surfaces from knife cuts.

Always wear goggles when using sharp tools or machinery.

Research

Research means finding information that will help you to design and manufacture your product. Project research is done for many reasons. It lets you find out what has been done before, what works and what does not. Research is always important in design technology. Without it you may find it difficult to form design ideas and move your project forward.

Research can be carried out in lots of different ways, using a variety of sources of information, including:

- books, magazines and CD-Roms
- the Internet
- television
- shops
- people who use products.

We will look at five areas of research that will help you to design and make mechanical projects:

- products and **mechanisms**
- product **analysis**
- users
- materials and **components**
- equipment.

Researching products and mechanisms

An important stage of project research is to study examples of existing products and mechanisms. You will need to investigate them to learn how they work. Look at bicycles, for example, which are made up of many different mechanisms. The brakes are a lever mechanism, the pedals turn a **crank** mechanism, while the crank is attached to a chain and **sprocket** mechanism.

chain and sprocket   crank   pedal   brake lever

The designer of a bicycle uses several different mechanisms to make it work properly. Some of these mechanisms are shown in the picture. You could study a bicycle to see exactly how they work together.

Types of mechanism

The following are the main types of mechanisms it will be useful for you to look at in your research. A more comprehensive list of mechanisms and the jobs that they do can be found on pages 44–45. Try modelling some basic mechanisms in card. This will help you to understand how the mechanisms work and will help you to choose a mechanism that matches the needs of your product.

Levers and linkages

A lever is a rigid rod that turns about a fixed **axis** called a **fulcrum** or a **pivot**. A **linkage** is used to join different parts of a mechanism together in order for them to move in a certain way.

Crank and slider

A **crank** is a stiff arm that connects to a shaft and will apply **torque** to that shaft. A slider is a sliding part of a mechanism that is connected to a crank by a linkage.

Belts and pulleys

A pulley is a wheel with a grooved rim. A belt is used to connect two pulleys together.

Gears

A gear is made of gear wheels that mesh together. A gear's purpose is to transmit **rotary** motion and force. A group of gears is called a gear train.

Rack and pinion

A rack is a straight-toothed bar that meshes with a **pinion**, a toothed wheel. They are used to transfer rotary motion into **linear** motion or vice versa.

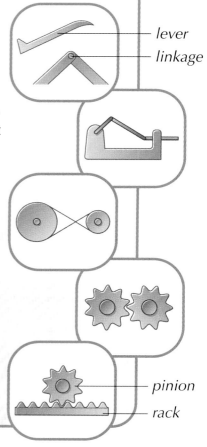

lever
linkage

pinion
rack

Researching users

Collecting information about what people want from a particular product is a very important area of research. This information can be gathered in two ways:

- Personal interviews – interviewing people individually is an excellent method of gathering specific information in detail.
- Questionnaires – a questionnaire is a form with a number of questions that relate to a product. People fill in the form and return the answers to the designer. The most difficult part is writing the questions. Once you have come up with good questions, the questionnaire can be distributed to people in the **target market**, and later collected and analysed.

Both of these methods are effective in gathering information from people, and can of course be used together.

Product analysis

Product **analysis** involves looking at things (observing) and thinking about them (analysing). It is where designers look at an existing product that is similar to the one they want to make.

In the course of **researching** a project, you will need to collect pictures and research data on existing similar products. You will need to examine the information you find in detail. This can give you valuable insights to how methods and materials are best used. Good design brings together and uses a lot of information. You will need to develop skills to solve each 'design and make' problem as you come across it.

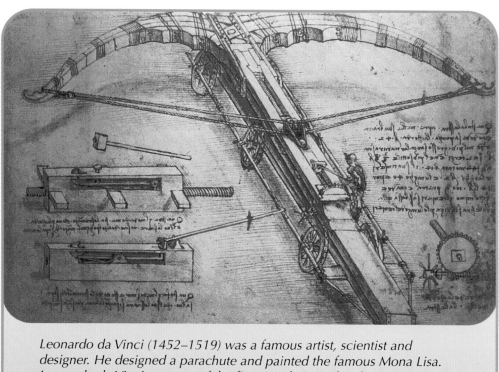

Leonardo da Vinci (1452–1519) was a famous artist, scientist and designer. He designed a parachute and painted the famous Mona Lisa. Leonardo da Vinci was one of the first people to realize how important product analysis is. Leonardo learned a lot about things by observation and analysis. This picture shows his design drawing for a giant catapult.

Writing a product analysis

Follow these steps when doing product analysis:

1 Look carefully at the product you wish to analyse. Sketch it from various angles (above, side on, beneath). Alternatively, use pictures or photographs of the product.

2 Next add comments about what you see. Make notes with arrows pointing to the part of the product each comment is related to. This is called annotation.

Use the headings in the table opposite as a basis for your annotation. Each heading is about a **characteristic** of the product you are analysing. On the picture or sketch you have made of the product, ask and answer questions about each of its characteristics.

Characteristic	Description
Colour	Colour can make things appear bright or dull, warm or cold, exciting or boring. We associate colour with emotion. Different colours appeal to different ages and genders. What age and gender (male or female) is the product for?
Materials	Materials can be soft, hard, durable (hard wearing), strong, water resistant, weak, flexible, heavy, light. What materials is the product made of?
Shape	2D objects have shape (such as a triangle or circle). 3D objects have form (like a pyramid or sphere). What is the best shape for your product?
Size	Is the size of the product important? If so, in what way is it important?
Patterns	What patterns (if any) are visible on your product? What effect do they have on it?
Textures	Texture is the way a surface feels (smooth, rough, hard, soft, gooey). What textures have been used on the product? What effect do they have?
Aesthetics	Aesthetics are concerned with how good a product looks. Is the product attractive? Does it need to be?
Symmetry	Our brains like pictures and objects that look balanced. **Symmetrical** objects are balanced; they are the same on both sides. Non-symmetrical objects are different on each side. Is the product symmetrical or non-symmetrical?
Style	Style is concerned with the look of the object. It could be modern or traditional, for example. Does the product have a style?
Function	Function is concerned with what a product will do. For example, the primary function of a mobile phone is to make and receive phone calls. Its secondary function is to send and receive text messages. What function does your product serve?
Market	All products are sold in the open market to people who buy them, called **consumers**. Products can be aimed at different markets and people. What age group or type of person is the product aimed at?

Materials and components

In order to make a mechanical construction, you will need to decide what types of **resistant materials** are best suited to your design. **Mechanisms** can also be made using plastic, but in this book we will just be using wood, metal or card.

When choosing materials to make your mechanism you need to consider some basic questions:

What properties will the materials need in order to make the design successful?

Physical **properties** control what a material can do. For example, a tough material will cope with blows without breaking, whereas a **brittle** material will be easily broken. Other properties to consider include strength, flexibility, weight and size.

What appearance do I want it to have?

Different materials will have different surface finishes, such as rough, smooth, textured or coloured and so on.

What material is available?

Materials will need to be readily available. It is pointless specifying a material that has little availability and that is very expensive, such as gold or titanium.

What materials can I afford?

Materials need to be within your budget. You may have to avoid specifying (choosing) some of the more expensive materials and components, such as brass and jelutong.

Resistant material	Properties	Advantages/ disadvantages	Cost	Uses
Timber				
Red deal (pine)	Softwood	Easy to cut and shape	Low	Frameworks, furniture, toys
Jelutong	Hardwood	Very easy to cut and shape, no knots	High	Model making, doors, drawing boards

Resistant material	Properties	Advantages/ disadvantages	Cost	Uses
Manufactured boards				
Plywood (interior grade)	Tough	Easier to finish than exterior grade	Low	Drawers, toys, mechanical parts, furniture
Plywood (exterior grade)	Tough, waterproof	Can split when cut	Medium	Roof cladding, floors
MDF	Hard, keeps edges well	Shapes and decorates well, but generates fine dust when cut	Low	kitchens, toys, tables, furniture, floorboards
Manufactured rods				
Dowel	Soft, cylinder shaped wood	Cuts easily	Low	Toys, jointing, furniture, decoration
Metals				
Aluminium	Silver colour, soft metal, does not rust	Easy to cut and shape, polishes well; difficult to join using heat	Medium	Decorative items, casting, car bodies
Brass	Gold colour, tarnishes slowly	Easy to join using heat, polishes well	High	Mechanical parts, door handles, decorative items, hinges
Mild steel	Grey colour, rusts easily without protection	Easy to join using heat; difficult to cut and shape	Low	Mechanical parts, frameworks, bicycles, car bodies
Components				
Screws	Brass or metal	Easy to fit, to form a temporary fixing	Low	Many uses
Ratchet rivets	Clear plastic	Easy to fix together, to form a temporary fixing	Medium	Rotating joints

Equipment

Once you have decided on the materials you require, you will have to select the correct tools and equipment for the job. You will require tools that will allow you to:

- measure and mark out your design accurately
- hold work in place
- cut your material to size
- make holes in your material
- join parts of your material
- clean up your material
- apply a finish to your material.

Which tools should I use?

This table shows the tools and equipment you need for measuring and marking out designs in a range of **resistant materials**.

Examples of equipment you will need for making the projects in this book.

Process	Material			
	Card/paper	**Wood**	**Metal**	**Plastic**
Measurement	Plastic 30 cm ruler	Metal 30 cm ruler	Metal 30 cm ruler	Metal 30 cm ruler
Marking out	HB pencil	HB pencil	**Scriber**	Scriber or felt-pen
Marking out right angles	30/60° set square	Try-square	Engineer's square	Engineer's square
Marking out angles	180° protractor	180° protractor	180° protractor	180° protractor
Marking out irregular shapes	Card template	Card template	Card template	Card template
Holding	Masking tape or G-clamp	Woodwork vice or G-clamp	Metalwork vice or G-clamp	Metalwork vice or G-clamp

Process	Material			
	Card/paper	Wood	Metal	Plastic
Cutting Cutting straight lines	Craft knife	Tenon saw	Hacksaw	Hacksaw
Cutting curved lines	Craft knife, scissors	Coping saw, fret saw	Tin-snips, abrasive file	Coping saw, fret saw
Trimming Trimming straight edges	Craft knife	Plane, flat file, belt sander	Guillotine, flat file	Flat file, belt sander
Trimming curved edges	Craft knife	Surform, round file	Round file	Round file
Making holes	Hole punch	Hand drill, pillar drill	Hand drill, pillar drill	Hand drill, pillar drill
Making slots	Craft knife	Morticer, drill, chisel, mallet	**Milling** machine, drill, file	Milling machine, drill, file
Making rebates	Laminating card sections	Tenon saw and chisel, rebate plane, plough plane, router	Milling machine	Milling machine
Bending	Straight edge and hand	Flexible plywood and jig	Vice and mallet	Strip heater
Joining Temporary	Paper fasteners, tape, adhesive tape	Screws	Screws, nuts, bolts	Screws, ratchet rivets
Permanent		Adhesive tape, panel pins, nails	Rivets	Adhesive tape
Cleaning up	Rubber (eraser)	Glass paper	Wet & dry paper, emery cloth	Wet & dry paper, buffing machine
Finishes	Plastic film **laminate**	Varnish, wax, paint	Paint, lacquer	Polish

Design specifications explained

What does a specification do?

A design **specification** describes in simple sentences what you intend your product to be like and what you hope to achieve. It is often separated into a user specification (what it must do to satisfy the people who want it) and a manufacturing specification (how it will be made and to what quality). It should be very easy to understand.

When do I do a specification?

A design specification is done after you have completed your project **research** and product **analysis**, but before you write down your initial design ideas.

Why do I need a specification?

A specification sets out the targets, or **criteria**, that you have identified for your product. The targets need to be clear and easily understood by other people. When you **evaluate** your product you will need to refer to the specification to see if the final outcome meets the targets set out in the original specification.

What does a specification look like?

A specification is best presented as a series or table of statements. The statements can be open or fixed in nature. Do not write a descriptive paragraph, like a story, though.

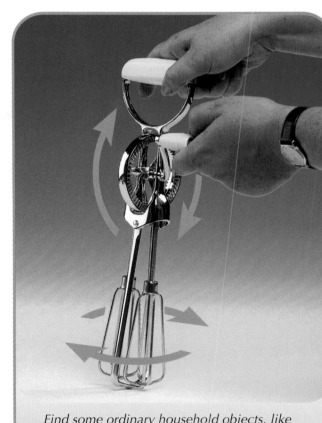

Find some ordinary household objects, like this hand whisk, and practise creating design specifications for them. This whisk is light, easy to maintain and it withstands regular use.

What type of statement?

Specification statements can be fixed, semi-fixed or open in nature. An example of each would be:

- Open statement – My product can be any colour.

- Semi-fixed statement – My product will be a bright primary colour.

- Fixed statement – My product will be coloured red.

Specification statements will be required for all aspects of the product. The table below gives some example statements that you might use if you were writing a design specification for a chair for a young child.

Criteria	Statement
Main function of the product	My product will seat a three-year-old child comfortably.
Other functions of the product	My product will act as a rocking chair.
Size	My product will be small in size.
Weight	My product should be as light as possible.
Durability	My product should withstand regular use.
Materials	My product will be made from a combination of materials.
Appearance/shape	My product will be appealing to young children.
Style/form	My product will be in the form of an animal.
Colour/texture	My product will use a range of smooth gloss colours.
Market	My product is aimed at the infant market.
Manufacturing cost	My product will cost approximately £5 ($A13) to make.
Selling price	My product will sell for about £15 ($A39).
Maintenance	My product will be maintenance free (easy to look after).
Safety	My product will have no sharp edges or small parts.
Where it is used	My product will be able to be used indoors.
Construction time	My product will be made in 16 workshop hours.
Environmental issues	My product will use an economical amount of material.
Manufacturing	My product should lend itself to mass production.
Quality	My product will be of high quality.

Design ideas and development

Once you have completed your **research** and created a design **specification**, it is time to come up with some design ideas. The first stage in creating designs is to sketch a number of different ideas. These should show what you want your product to look like and what it will do. Remember you are intending to design and make a product using an existing type of **mechanism**, not to invent a totally new type of mechanism!

For each sketch idea you will need to:

- show the subject of your idea (the theme), such as a car or an animal, presented in an attractive way
- show what the product does: for example, how it moves, and in what direction.

It is best at this stage to show how the product moves by drawing arrows rather than attempting to draw the product and its mechanism actually working. For example, you may wish to show a handle turning that causes something to pop up. You would show this with a curved arrow. The illustration below shows how you might sketch a design for a barking dog toy.

Look at all the options

When you are sketching, you may have some initial ideas that later turn out to be too complicated to make. That does not matter, because at this stage you should be looking at all the possible design options.

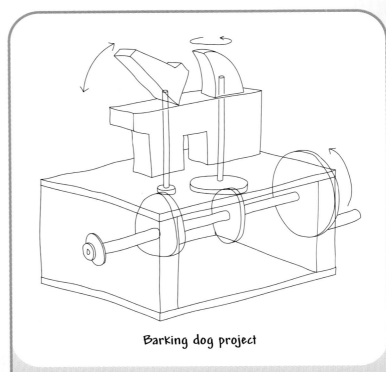

Barking dog project

This sketch shows a design idea for the barking dog toy (see pages 40–43). Arrows are used to show how the main parts move.

How to refine and develop designs

You now need to develop one of your design ideas. Choose your favourite idea from the sketches you have made. At this stage you should have decided exactly how you want your product to perform.

The next stage is to consider the types of motion you require. You will need to decide what type of movement you want going into the mechanism (the input) and what movement you wish to see happen (the **output**).

The best way to explain and label how the mechanism works is to break the design down into a simple system, like this:

> **Input → process → output**

- The input is the motion that goes into the mechanism to make it move, for example turning (rotating) a handle.
- The process is the mechanism type, for example gears.
- The output is the motion the mechanism creates, for example turning (rotating) in a different direction.

The input and the output are the easiest parts of the system. It is usually more difficult to choose the mechanism type that will make it happen. The mechanism property chart on pages 44–45 shows the types of mechanism you can use to change one type of movement (the input) to another (the output). Once you have decided on the type of mechanism that suits your design idea, then you will need to adapt it to fit your own design specification. This may mean changing its size or where it is positioned on your design, for example.

The design drawing

You should now finalize your design drawing, labelling the parts clearly and including information about the materials you will be using. You will use this drawing to help plan how your product will be made.

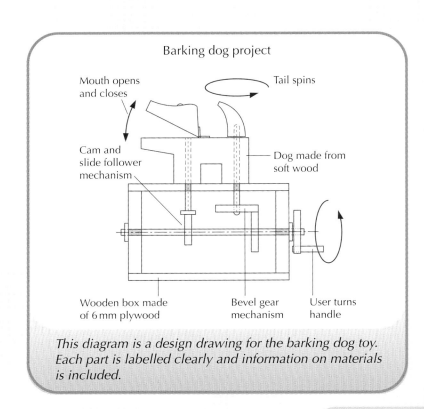

Barking dog project

Mouth opens and closes

Tail spins

Cam and slide follower mechanism

Dog made from soft wood

Wooden box made of 6 mm plywood

Bevel gear mechanism

User turns handle

This diagram is a design drawing for the barking dog toy. Each part is labelled clearly and information on materials is included.

Preparing and planning for manufacture

There are several stages in planning and preparing to make a product. The first step is to make a **prototype** of your design. A prototype is a model that is used to check that a design will work. It is made from materials that are cheap and easy to use, such as card. This is because it is a good idea to make **modifications** and correct any mistakes to your design before you spend lots of time making a very precise (and possibly expensive) product that does not work!

Once you have refined your design, you will be able to make the final product in the material you have chosen, such as a soft wood.

Your preparation should also include checking that you have the tools and materials that you need to do the job properly.

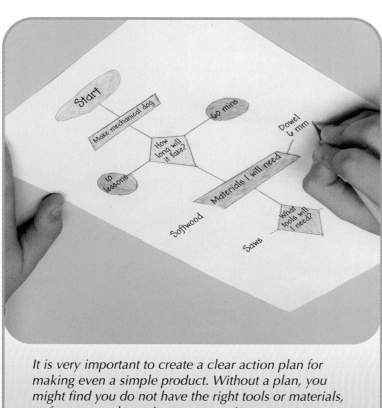

It is very important to create a clear action plan for making even a simple product. Without a plan, you might find you do not have the right tools or materials, or forget to make an important part!

Writing an action plan

It is important to write an action plan to help you with manufacturing your product. By breaking the task down into stages it will appear less complex. Your plan will include several stages, and should have a description under each of the headings listed on the table on page 21. You will find action plans like this in the projects on pages 26–43.

Some designers use **flowcharts** to plan how to manufacture a product. A flowchart is pictured on page 21. It is best to use a flowchart for each section of the whole process, rather than trying to show everything in one big chart.

Action plan

Action plan headings	Example description
1 The action, which is a clear statement of what you intend to do at each stage.	I will cut the straight edges with a Tenon saw.
2 A list of the materials you will need, with an estimated size.	Plywood – 150 mm long x 150 mm wide x 6 mm thick Softwood – 100 mm long x 50 mm wide x 21 mm thick
3 A list of the tools and equipment you will use.	Tenon saw Pillar drill
4 An estimate of the time it will take to carry out each stage.	20 minutes
5 A section to note any modifications you make. This is very important as it will help when you **evaluate** your product. Make notes on what worked, what you needed to change and how you changed it.	I used thicker plywood so that the **mechanism** support would not bend.

Flowchart symbols

A flowchart is made up of the steps in a process, connected by arrows to show where to go to the next step. Flowcharts use special symbols to show what sort of activity has to be done:

- Ovals – an oval symbol is used to show the start and end of a flowchart
- Diamonds – a diamond shows that a decision needs to be made
- Rectangles – rectangles are used to show actions.

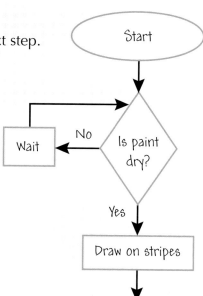

Evaluation

Evaluation is something you do every day, probably without even realizing it! For example you may evaluate what shoes to buy or food to eat. Your decision will be based on a number of **criteria**. These criteria are similar to **specification** criteria.

The purpose of evaluation is to improve on what you have done before. Therefore evaluation is a continual process. Throughout the designing, developing and making processes you should keep on evaluating your product, and changing it if necessary.

How to do a final evaluation

A final evaluation is a review of your finished product. You will need to use your judgement to assess the outcome of the design. Evaluation can be broken down into three stages, each of which is discussed below.

These two pupils are evaluating the mechanical spider toy (see page 36). They are checking its quality and build – two important aspects of evaluation.

1 Checking your outcomes against the original specification

Read through your original specification. Now decide if you managed to achieve each point in your specification. The specification outlines how you intended your product to turn out, and this may have changed over the course of the design process.

- If you did achieve the specification point, for example that the durability is good, you need to say how this has been achieved.

- If you did not manage to achieve a specification point, say why it was not achieved, or why it was changed. If changes were made, say how successful they were.

You can write up your assessment of the product as a table like this one:

Specification point	Question	Answer
Colour: My product will be yellow and blue.	Did the product turn out to be yellow and blue?	No, it was clear that just using yellow and blue was not going to create the right effect. I changed my design and used a range of colours to much better effect. The result was a much more attractive and marketable design.
Size: My product will be small.	Have you kept the product small?	Yes, I managed to keep the product to a hand-held size although it did turn out larger than I had originally intended. This change in size affected the cost of the product but allowed for more detailed design features.

2 Consumer testing

Consumer testing is getting people who might use the product to test it.

- Find out what they think is good about the product (its strengths), and *why* it is good.
- Find out what they think is poor about the product (its weaknesses) and *how* and *why* the product needs to change.

Write up the consumers' comments in a logical way. You may add comments to support other people's views or comments that argue against their views. (This may help you identify strengths and weaknesses in the product to help you with part 3.)

3 Identifying the strengths and weaknesses of your product

State what you consider to be the strengths of your product and give reasons. Then suggest possible **modifications** and improvements for the weaknesses you have identified.

Industrial study: Cabaret Mechanical Theatre

The Cabaret Mechanical Theatre is not a theatre or a cabaret, exhibition or museum; it is a collection of automata. **Automaton** is the word for a moving mechanical sculpture. Automata is the plural of automaton. The CMT has many of these enchanting mechanical toys.

Early days

The Theatre started life in 1979 as a crafts shop, called Cabaret, in Falmouth, Cornwall. It was opened by Sue Jackson and sold simple wooden toys, made by Peter Markey, alongside knitwear and ceramics. The growing collection of mechanical automata was popular with customers. It was clear that people would pay to bring automata to life. In May 1983, still in Falmouth, the Cabaret Mechanical Theatre was set up, and customers now paid to turn the handles and press the buttons.

This is an automata called Barecats, created by Paul Spooner and Matt Smith. When the handle at the back of the base is turned, the large barecat moves. The mechanism also turns the smaller handle, though it looks as if the larger barecat is doing the work. The head, arm and legs of the smaller barecat move.

The collection

The collection was largely made up of small hand-**cranked** pieces by artists Peter Markey and Paul Spooner. For protection, most of them were put in cases and motorized so that they could be operated by push button. Some people bought pieces, and larger one-off machines were created.

Each artist works in their own way. Most can take their first ideas straight to a **prototype** or finished piece. Some artists, such as Keith Newstead, put their basic ideas on paper first.

An artist like Paul Spooner will typically take about two weeks to make a piece, though he might take several months to complete a complicated design. He works in a process of continual development, making an item then throwing it away to make an improved version. Peter Markey, who is in his seventies, sometimes makes several small pieces in a day!

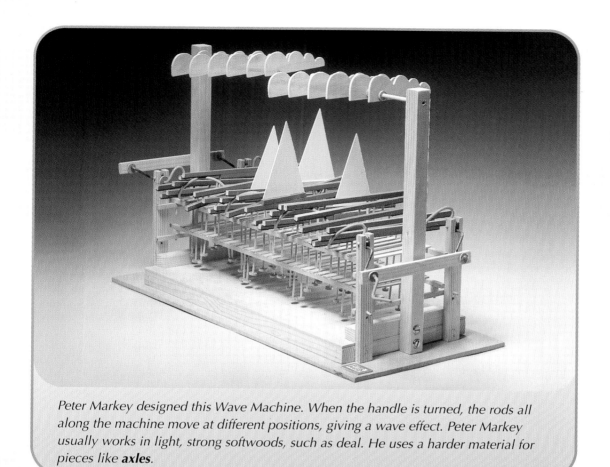

*Peter Markey designed this Wave Machine. When the handle is turned, the rods all along the machine move at different positions, giving a wave effect. Peter Markey usually works in light, strong softwoods, such as deal. He uses a harder material for pieces like **axles**.*

Many of the automata are very complex, with lots of movement. However, they are all made using basic, simple **mechanisms** that anyone can use in their own designs.

CMT today

As the collection grew, it became obvious that the exhibition was growing too large to stay in the shop in Cornwall. In 1985, Cabaret Mechanical Theatre opened in Covent Garden, London, with new work by Tim Hunkin and, a little later, Michael Howard. Today, nearly all of the work in the Cabaret Mechanical Theatre is of a humorous, entertaining and educational nature. As well as smaller machines, there are about 20 coin-operated, larger scale automata.

CMT is involved in many educational projects with schools in the UK. Sue Jackson herself shows students how food can be used in making a mechanism – have you ever thought of using a ginger nut biscuit as a **cam**? There have also been exhibitions in Japan and Europe. The collection continues to grow.

At the time of writing, the Theatre is in the process of moving to a new home. You can find out more about the collection using the contact details on page 47.

Project 1: V-fold pop-up card

The design brief

A small local company that designs and makes greetings cards has asked you to design and make a greetings card for a special occasion. The card will have a 'pop-up' design inside.

Product specification

The product **specification** is a list of things your product must be or do:

- the product will be made from white card, ideally A4, 220 **gsm**
- the maximum size of the product is to be A4 when open, A5 when closed
- the product will use a V-fold type mechanical pop-up
- the product must be safe for users and all small children
- the product should withstand reasonable multiple use
- the product should be aesthetically pleasing (look good).

A V-fold pop-up card – a pop-up cat.

Research

Research the following areas to help you to develop your product by, firstly, doing some product **analysis**. Identify and analyse any existing pop-up cards that are similar to the one that you are developing. You could look in shops or even on company websites on the Internet. You could also look at various designs of V-fold **mechanisms**.

The resources needed for this project.

Resources

Materials and components

- base card, A4, 220 gsm or 160 gsm
- thick white card, A4, ideally 220 gsm
- double-sided sticky tape or glue

Tools and equipment

- craft knife or scissors
- cutting board
- 30 cm ruler
- 180° protractor, set square, compass
- pencil
- coloured pencils or pens
- scoring pencil

Design ideas

1 When designing a pop-up it is important to have a theme, such as a house or vehicle. With greetings cards you will want to find a theme to please the person who will receive the card.

2 When working on new designs, make a rough paper version first. This will allow you to check that all the pieces fit and fold together correctly.

3 Decorate the design before the pieces are folded or glued into place.

4 Decorate around the pop-up, as well as the pop-up itself.

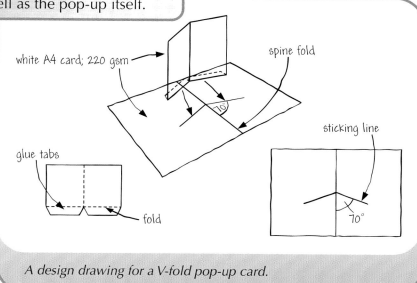

white A4 card; 220 gsm

spine fold

sticking line

glue tabs

fold

70°

A design drawing for a V-fold pop-up card.

Hints for success

! On the base, the V-fold must be connected at an angle (about 70 degrees) from the central horizontal spine fold.

! The central fold of the pop-up must be in line with the central spine fold of the card when it is fixed.

! As the card closes, the pop-up will fold down backwards, away from the viewer. Check that the pop-up does not stick out of the top of the card when flat. If it does, move the pop-up nearer to the base of the card before you fix it.

! Score all fold lines: this will make the fold more accurate.

! Accuracy is very important – check your work so that the pop-up will fold away cleanly.

! Glue tabs should be positioned so that they fold back and are hidden from view by the pop-up piece.

Action plan

Using the following steps to produce an action plan of how you are going to manufacture your pop-up card. Do allow enough time for any glue to dry.

Action	Resources
1 Locate the centre of the card. Take the A4 base card and draw a light diagonal line from each corner forming a cross in the centre. This is the centre point of the card.	• 30 cm ruler • Pencil • A4 card
2 Score and fold your A4 base card in half down its centre, forming a spine. Open out the card.	• 30 cm ruler • Scoring pencil • Cutting board
3 Hold a protractor along the spine fold line, locating the centre of the protractor at the centre point of the card. Mark a line at 70 degrees, connect this to the centre point of the card. Repeat on the other side. This is where the V-fold pop-up is to be located.	• 180° protractor • Pencil
4 Mark out the V-fold pop-up design on a second piece of card. Allow 20 mm for glue tabs. Its maximum size should be 220 mm wide x 130 mm high (including glue tabs).	• Ruler • Pencil • Card
5 Cut out the pop-up piece to shape. Decorate your piece using coloured pencils or pens. Score and fold down its centre (ensuring front design is on the inside of the fold).	• Coloured pencils or pens • Scoring pencil • Cutting board
6 Open out pop-up, score and fold the glue tabs. Cut the tab sides at a 45 degree angle from the centre line fold (to allow for movement).	• Pencil • Protractor • Scoring pencil • Craft knife • Cutting board
7 Apply glue to the rear of the right-hand-side glue tab on the pop-up. Place the right-hand-side pop-up glue tab onto the previously marked out line on the right hand side of the base card. Hold down, letting the glue take hold.	• Glue • Card
8 Fold the pop-up piece into its position, then apply glue to the left glue tab.	• Glue • Card
9 Close the base card over it and the left glue tab will locate its best position! Apply pressure to the card to ensure glue takes hold.	• Card
10 Test the product; open and close the card to check the pop-up works.	• Product
11 Complete any **modifications**.	• Product

1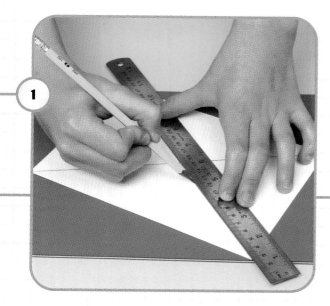

5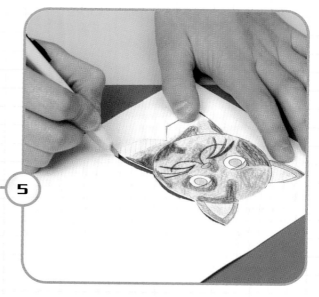

7

8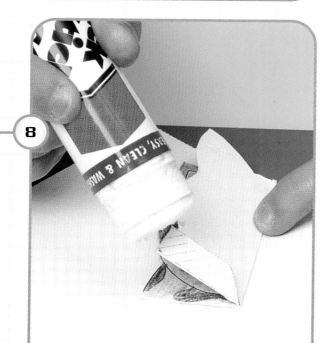

Evaluation

Answer the following questions about your product to help you **evaluate** how your product development went:

1 Am I pleased with my finished product?
2 In what ways could I make my product better?
3 Did I use my time effectively? In what ways?
4 Was my design work of a good standard?
5 Could my design work be better?
6 What do other people think of my work?
7 What parts of the project did I find difficult and why?
8 Did I enjoy the project?

Project 2: Development of the V-fold

This project develops the basic idea of Project 1, the V-fold pop-up card, but gives you ideas that are a little more complicated to make. Use the action plan on page 28 as a basis for making these products. Note: In all pictures shown, lines that should be cut appear as solid black, while fold lines appear as dotted lines.

Multiple pop-ups

You can add depth to your pop-up by adding extra pop-up layers. With a number of pieces popping up you must ensure the pieces do not clash when the card is closed. To avoid this, the front pop-up should fold back less than the pop-ups behind it, or all pop-ups should fold parallel to each other. Also, if you make the angle between the spine and the fixed tab smaller, the piece will lean back less as the base closes.

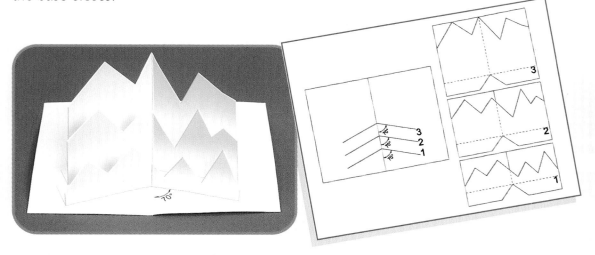

Forward V-fold

A forward V-fold is the reverse of the V-fold. In this case, the pop-up folds towards the viewer as the card is closed. Tall pop-up pieces must be positioned near the top of the card. This method leaves more space for text and images in front of the pop-up.

You will need to alter the design of the pop-up base if the design is to work. The angle at the base must be 80 degrees. If it is 90, the pop-up will sag forward unless the base is perfectly flat.

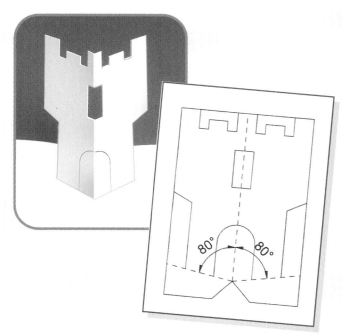

V-fold with cuts and creases

Shapes can be developed to look more three-dimensional (3D) by adding two **symmetrical** creases and cuts. The design must be the same on both sides to work. The cuts must be placed symmetrically across the fold line of the pop-up. Crease lines are connected symmetrically to the end of cuts to create shapes. This method will require experimentation, and so it is a good idea to plan and try your ideas on paper first.

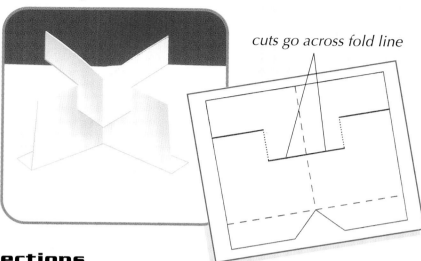

cuts go across fold line

V-fold with projections

Projecting parts for shapes can be made by making cuts that start and finish on the pop-up's central crease line. The shape is drawn from the central fold and cut before the central fold is made.

Make sure the cut starts and ends on the central fold line, and that the fold line does not cross the projection. Extra detail can be added by fixing additional pieces to the projections.

cuts start and finish on fold line

> **Tips to help you make these projects**

! Do not draw the projections too large on the pop-up.
! Take extra care when cutting and folding.
! Cut lines are shown as a solid, continuous black line.
! Fold lines are shown as a dotted black line.

Project 3: A themed mechanical display

The design brief

A small local company that makes mechanical displays has asked you to design and make a themed mechanical display. The display must be operated using a **crank** and slider **mechanism**, and can be manufactured using card or wood.

Product specification

The product **specification** is a list of things your product must be or do:

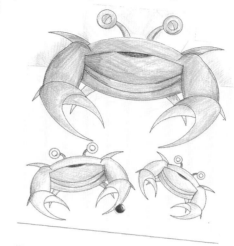

- the display will feature a **reciprocating** motion
- the product will use a crank and slider mechanism
- the product will be made from thick card
- the maximum size of the product is 150 mm high x 150 mm wide
- the product must be safe for users
- the product should last and withstand regular use
- the product should be aesthetically pleasing (look good).

This finished mechanical display is made of card. The theme is seaside life.

Research

Identify and **analyse** any existing products that are similar to the one that you are developing. You could look in toyshops or even in museums that have displays of mechanical toys.

The resources you will need to make this project.

Resources

Materials and components
- A4 card, 220 **gsm** or 160 gsm
- 15 mm paper fasteners
- clear sticking tape

Tools and equipment
- scissors and craft knife
- cutting board
- hole punch
- pencil
- 30 cm plastic ruler
- scoring pencil
- coloured pencils

Design ideas

1 First do a quick **brainstorm** in order to find subjects or themes for your display. This will help to give you inspiration for design ideas.

2 Sketch a range of different shapes but keep them simple.

3 Once you have selected the best idea, show how you hope it will move and in what way – use arrows drawn onto your sketch.

4 From your research you will be able to choose a mechanism for the type of movement you want to create. Put this into a **mechanical systems** box to show the

input ➔ process ➔ output

for each mechanism to be used. See the mechanism property chart on pages 44–45 for help.

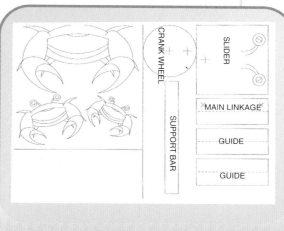

The design drawing for the mechanical crab display.

5 Sketch what you think the mechanism will look like. You can change this at a later time if it is not right.

Hints for success

- ! Keep your ideas simple. Some of the best ideas are not complex, but still very effective.
- ! When using mechanisms allow for errors and corrections. To help get sizes right make a card **prototype**. This will save time when it comes to making in wood.

- ! Always double-check your marking out and measurement when making mechanisms. A small error could lead to the mechanism not working.
- ! Take your time and have patience – mechanisms are fiddly.

Action plan

Use the following steps as the basis for your action plan:

Action	Resources	Time needed
1 Take a piece of A4 card and cut it in half. One piece will form the stand, the other the **mechanism's** mechanical parts.	• A4 card • Scissors • 30 cm ruler	1 min
2 Mark out the design of the display on to the surface of one piece of card and colour it. Maximum size 150 mm x 150 mm. Leave a space 150 mm x 60 mm at the bottom to form the base stand.	• Ruler • Pencil and coloured pencils • Card	10 mins
3 Mark out the mechanical parts on to the second piece of card. You will need: slider (80 mm x 80 mm); circular **crank** wheel (60mm diameter); main linkage (80 mm x 15 mm); two guide supports for the slider (80 mm x 30 mm); support bar (130 mm x 15 mm). Make sure that the slider is decorated to fit in with the main card.	• Card • Pencil • Ruler • Coloured pencils	20 mins
4 Cut out the mechanical parts with a craft knife (or scissors).	• Craft knife • Cutting board • Ruler	20 mins
5 Take the two guide supports, score and fold them in half along the greatest length. Place the slider between them so you know how far apart they need to be. Use tape to fix the guides vertically and centrally at the top of the rear of the main card. (Ensure the slider can move easily.)	• Tape • Scoring pencil • Ruler	5 mins
6 Make holes at each end of the main **linkage** and at the bottom of the slider. Fix linkage and slider together with a paper fastener.	• Hole punch • Paper fastener	2 mins
7 Cut holes in the centre of the crank wheel and at its outer edge.	• Craft knife • Hole punch	2 mins
8 Cut a hole in the main card approximately 75 mm in from the left and 90 mm up from the bottom.	• Craft knife • Hole punch • Ruler, pencil	5 mins

4

Action	Resources	Time needed
9 Fix a paper fastener through the front of the main card. At the rear, fix the fastener through the centre of the crank wheel and through the other end of the main linkage (ensure wheel can rotate).	• Paper fastener	2 mins
10 Place the slider between the guides. Fold the guides over and secure with the support bar near the top of the main card. Fix with tape on each side to hold the slider in place.	• Tape	2 mins
11 Place a paper fastener through the outer hole of the crank wheel and turn. The crank and slider mechanism should move the slider in a **reciprocating** motion.	• Paper fastener	1 min
12 Test product and make adjustments as required.	• Product	5 mins

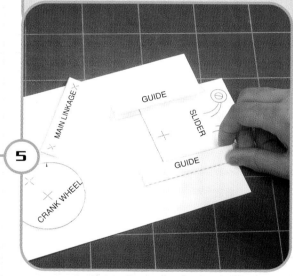

5

9

Evaluation

Answer the following questions about your product to help you **evaluate** how your product development went:

1 Am I pleased with my finished product?
2 In what ways could I make my product better?
3 Did I use my time effectively? In what ways?
4 Was my design work of a good standard?
5 Could my design work be better?
6 What do other people think of my work?
7 What parts of the project did I find difficult and why?
8 Did I enjoy the project?

11

Project 4: Mechanical spider

The design brief

A small local company that makes mechanical toys has asked you to design and make a mechanical toy in the form of an animal. The toy must be designed to be pushed along and contain levers and **linkage mechanisms**. It must be manufactured using wood.

This finished mechanical spider is made of wood with lever and linkage mechanisms.

Product specification

The product **specification** is a list of things your product must be or do:

- the product will move its legs only
- the product will be made from wood
- the maximum size of the product is to be 150 mm high x 150 mm wide
- the product will use lever and **linkage** mechanisms
- the product must be safe for users
- the product should last and withstand regular use
- the product should be aesthetically pleasing (look good).

Research

Research will help you to develop your product. Identify and **analyse** any existing products similar to the one that you are developing. Also, try investigating mechanisms that will produce the movement you require.

Some materials and components needed for this project.

Resources

Materials and components

- 6 mm plywood
- 6 mm dowel
- 15 mm softwood
- drawing pins
- foamex washers
- paint

Tools and equipment

- 30 cm metal ruler
- tenon saw
- fret saw
- hand or pillar drill
- 6.5 mm drill bit
- 50 mm hole saw

- belt sander
- needle files
- flat files
- brush
- coping saw
- abrasive paper
- pencil
- joggly eyes

Design ideas

1 First do a quick **brainstorm** in order to find subjects or themes for your product. This will help select an area of inspiration for design ideas.

2 Sketch a range of different animal shapes but keep them simple.

3 Once you have selected the best idea, show how you hope it will move and in what way – use arrows to indicate movement.

4 From your research you will be able to choose a mechanism for the type of movement you want to create. Put this into a **mechanical systems** box to show the

input ➔ process ➔ **output**

for each mechanism to be used. See the mechanism property chart on pages 44–45 for help.

5 Sketch what you think the mechanisms will look like. You can change the sketch at a later time if it is not right.

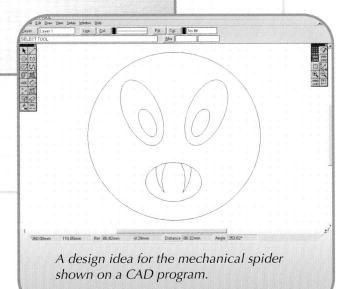

A design idea for the mechanical spider shown on a CAD program.

Hints for success

! Keep your ideas simple. Some of the best ideas are not complex, but still very effective.

! Always double-check your marking out and measurement when making mechanisms. A small error could lead to the mechanism not working.

! When using linkages, allow for errors and corrections. To help get sizes right make a card **prototype** model, which will save time when it comes to making in wood.

! Take your time and have patience, because mechanisms are fiddly to make successfully.

The following table is an action plan for manufacturing:

Action	Resources	Time needed
1 Mark out a horizontal base line 15 mm from the bottom of the plywood for the main body. From this base line mark out a centrally positioned rectangle on the body 100 mm wide, 50 mm high. Drill one at each corner of the rectangle.	• 6 mm plywood • Ruler, pencil • Hand drill/ pillar drill • 6.5 mm drill bit	10 mins
2 Mark out design of spider's head and body on to surface of your wood. The design must go around all of the four holes already drilled.	• 6 mm plywood • 15 mm softwood • Ruler, pencil	10 mins
3 Use a coping saw or fret saw to cut any curved edges to shape.	• Coping saw/ fret saw	20 mins
4 Smooth edges with belt sander, flat files and needle files. Finish with abrasive paper.	• Belt sander • Flat files, needle files • Abrasive paper	20 mins
5 Mark out and drill four wheels from the 15 mm softwood. Use a 50 mm hole saw in the pillar drill to do this.	• Ruler, pencil • Pillar drill • 50 mm hole saw • 15 mm softwood	10 mins
6 Mark out and drill one hole through each wheel. Locate this hole half way between the wheel's edge and the centre.	• Ruler, pencil • Hand drill/ pillar drill • 6.5 mm drill bit	5 mins
7 Mark out and cut 4 dowel rods each to 50 mm length. These will support the four wheels and upper leg **linkages**.	• 6 mm dowel • Fret saw • Pencil, ruler	5 mins
8 Push the 50 mm long dowel through the two lower holes in the body. Fix two wheels to each side of the body. Secure with drawing pins.	• 6 mm dowel • Drawing pins	2 mins
9 The mechanism's legs are each made of two linkages. Mark out length of the linkages: four linkages at 70 mm long and four linkages at 60 mm long. (Each leg is made of a connected 70 mm linkage and 60 mm linkage.) Cut them out.	• Ruler, pencil • Tenon saw • 15 mm x 15 mm softwood	10 mins

Action	Resources	Time needed
10 Drill two holes 40 mm apart in each 60 mm linkage. Drill two holes 50 mm apart in each 70 mm linkage.	• Pillar drill • 6.5 mm drill bit	10 mins
11 Mark out and cut eight dowel rods each to 35 mm length. These will form connections for the leg linkages.	• 6 mm dowel • Fret saw	5 mins
12 Fix 70 mm and 60 mm linkage together. Use 35 mm long dowel rod through one end of each linkage. Use two drawing pins to fix dowels. Repeat this for each leg. Fix the 70 mm linkage to a wheel using 35 mm long dowel. Fix with two drawing pins. Repeat for each of the four legs.	• Drawing pins • 6 mm dowel	10 mins
13 Using 50 mm long dowel, fix the top end of the linkage through the top hole in the body. Fix the wheel through the lower hole in the body.	• Drawing pins • 6 mm dowel	
14 Take apart toy and decorate product. Reassemble.	• Joggly eyes • Paint brush	20 mins
15 Test product and make fine adjustments.	• Product	5 mins

3

5

Do not forget to wear safety goggles when using the pillar drill.

10

14

Evaluation

Answer the following questions about your product to help you **evaluate** how your product development went:

1 Am I pleased with my finished product?
2 In what ways could I make my product better?
3 Did I use my time effectively? In what ways?
4 Was my design work of a good standard?
5 Could my design work be better?
6 What do other people think of my work?
7 What parts of the project did I find difficult and why?
8 Did I enjoy the project?

Project 5: Barking dog

The design brief

A small local company that makes mechanical toys has asked you to design and make a mechanical toy dog. The toy must be operated using a **mechanism** and manufactured using wood.

Product specification

The product **specification** is a list of things your product must be or do:

- the dog will move its mouth and tail
- the product will be made from wood
- the maximum size of the product is to be 150 mm high x 150 mm wide
- the product will use more than one type of mechanism
- the product must be safe for users
- the product should last and withstand regular use
- the product should be aesthetically pleasing (look good).

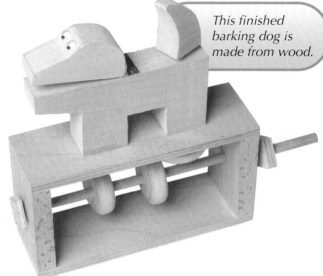

This finished barking dog is made from wood.

Research

Research will help you to develop your product. Identify and **analyse** any existing products similar to the one that you are developing. Also, investigate mechanisms that will produce the movement you require.

Some of the materials and components that are needed for this project.

Resources

Materials and components

- 21 mm jelutong or softwood
- 6 mm dowel
- 6 mm interior plywood or MDF
- **cam** and slide follower
- **bevel gear**
- tack pins
- PVA glue
- small brass hinge

Tools and equipment

- 30 cm metal ruler
- set square
- pencil
- tenon saw or band saw
- coping saw or fret saw
- hand or pillar drill
- 7 mm, 6.5 mm, 5.9 mm drill bits
- flat files
- needle files
- abrasive paper
- wood vice
- hammer

Design ideas

1 First do a quick **brainstorm** in order to find themes for your product. This will help select an area of inspiration for design ideas.

2 Sketch a range of different dog shapes but keep them simple – remember the mechanisms will need to be connected through the legs of the dog.

3 Once you have selected the best idea, show how you want it to move – use arrows to show the direction of movement.

4 From your research you will be able to choose mechanisms for the type of movement you want to create. Put them into a **mechanical systems** box to show the

input → process → **output**

for each mechanism to be used. See the mechanism property chart on pages 44–45 for help.

5 Sketch what you think each mechanism will look like. You can change this at a later time if it is not right.

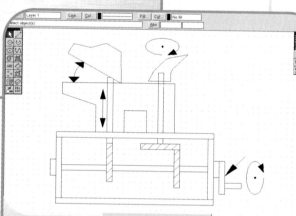

A design idea for the barking dog, shown on a CAD program.

Hints for success

! Keep ideas simple. Some of the best ideas are not complex, but still very effective.

! Always double-check your marking out and measurement when making mechanisms. A small error could lead to the mechanism not working.

! To find the centre of a square or rectangular piece of wood, draw straight diagonal lines joining opposite corners. Where they cross is the centre of the square or rectangle.

! Use **compression-fit** holes to avoid the need for glue.

! Holes that form a compression fit that will not allow movement should be sized 0.1 mm smaller in diameter than the size of the 6 mm dowel – i.e. 5.9 mm in diameter.

! Holes that allow sliding movement of the dowel parts to need to be larger in diameter by 1 mm than the 6 mm dowel – that is 7 mm in diameter.

! Take your time and have patience, because mechanisms are fiddly.

Action plan

Using the following action plan as a basis for making your own
mechanical dog:

Action	Resources	Time needed
1 Mark out the design of the dog on the surface of your wood. Mark out the four pieces of wood for the base.	• 21 mm softwood • Ruler, pencil • Set square	20 mins
2 Use a tenon saw to cut straight edges of your shapes to size.	• Tenon saw	10 mins
3 Use a coping saw or fret saw to cut any curved edges to shape.	• Coping saw/ fret saw	20 mins
4 Trim edges smooth with flat files and needle files. Finish with abrasive paper.	• Flat files, needle files • Abrasive paper	20 mins
5 Use PVA glue to fix the body of the dog centrally to the top of the base. Compress in a wood vice and wait for glue to set.	• PVA glue • Wood vice	10 mins
6 Mark out and drill two vertical holes through the body and each leg of the dog.	• Ruler, pencil • Hand drill/ pillar drill • 7 mm drill bit	5 mins
7 Mark out and drill two holes in the centre of both ends of the base.	• Ruler, pencil • Hand drill/ pillar drill • 7 mm drill bit	5 mins
8 Fix the base together with glue. Compress in a wood vice and wait for the glue to set.	• PVA glue • Wood vice	10 mins

1

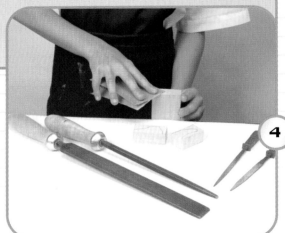

4

Action	Resources	Time needed
9 Drill compression holes in the **cam**, gear and bevel wheels. The hole in the cam wheel needs to be off centre.	• 5.9 mm drill bit • Cam, gear and bevel wheels	2 mins
10 Fix the cam and gear wheels to a horizontal dowel through the base. Fix the **bevel gear** to a dowel through the rear leg of the dog.	• 6 mm dowel • Cam, gear and bevel wheels • Bevel gear	10 mins
11 Align the mechanisms. Secure the horizontal dowel to the base with fixings cut from plywood.	• Hand drill/ pillar drill • 6.5 mm drill bit • 6 mm plywood	5 mins
12 Fix head to body using a hinge. Fix tail to rear vertical dowel using glue. Adjust dowels as required.	• Hinge • Pins, hammer • PVA glue • 6 mm dowels	5 mins
13 Test product and carry out modifications.	• Product	5 mins

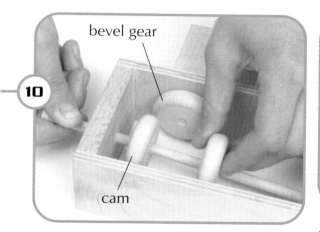

10

bevel gear

cam

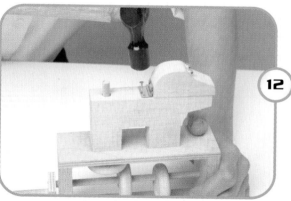

12

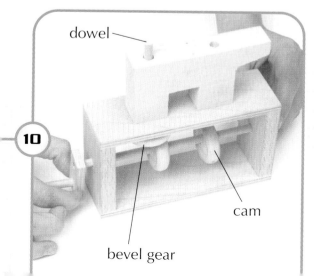

10

dowel

cam

bevel gear

Evaluation

Answer the following questions about your product to help you **evaluate** how your product development went:

1. Am I pleased with my finished product?
2. In what ways could I make my product better?
3. Did I use my time effectively? In what ways?
4. Was my design work of a good standard?
5. Could my design work be better?
6. What do other people think of my work?
7. What parts of the project did I find difficult and why?
8. Did I enjoy the project?

Mechanisms property chart

This chart shows what **mechanisms** you can use according to what sort of movement you want to create. It will help you with your design ideas in preparation for creating your projects.

To change movement from → to	You could use:		
Rotating → **Reciprocating** 	**Crank** and slider 	**Cam** and slide follower 	
Rotating → **Linear** 	Rack and **pinion** 	Chain and **sprocket** 	Screw thread 
Rotating → **Oscillating** 	Crank and slider 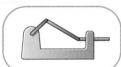	Cam and lever follower 	Peg and slot 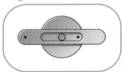
Reciprocating → Rotating 	Crank and slider 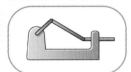		
Reciprocating → Oscillating 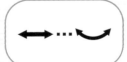	Crank and slider 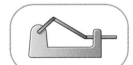	Rack and pinion 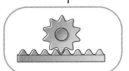	

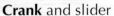

To change movement from → to

You could use:

Oscillating → Rotating

Crank and slider

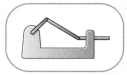

Peg and slot

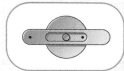

Wheel and **axle**

Oscillating → Reciprocating

Crank and slider

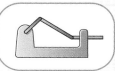

Cam and slide follower

Linear → Rotating

Rack and pinion

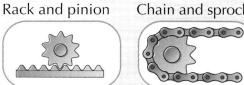

Chain and sprocket

Wheel and axle

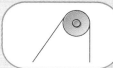

Left → Right

Levers

Linked levers

Rope and pulley

Horizontal → Vertical

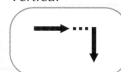

Levers

Linked levers

Rope and pulley

Change axis of rotation

Gears

Belt and pulley

Clockwise → Anticlockwise

Gears

Belt and pulley

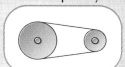

Glossary

analysis examining facts that you have gathered together about something and then thinking about them

automaton mechanical toy. The plural is automata.

axis point around which something moves

axle supporting shaft on which a wheel or wheels turn

bevel gear gear with wheels at right angles to each other

brainstorm quickly creating a number of different ideas

British Standard (BS) used to show a product conforms to a quality standard

brittle fragile material that will break easily

cam shaped wheel

characteristics particular features

components parts of a product

compression-fit when parts fit firmly together without using glue

consumer anybody who buys a product

crank wheel or linkage with turning handle

criteria various standards set on which you can make a judgement about something

design brief statement of what product is going to be made

evaluate/evaluation statements of what a designer thinks about a product and its manufacture

flowchart plan of action with different symbols to show different stages

fulcrum central pivot

gsm weight in grams per square metre

linear movement in a forward motion

linkage connection

mechanical system mechanism that contains an input, a process and an output

mechanism an object with moving parts

milling removal of material by a spinning tool bit in a horizontal way

modelling first 3D attempt at what a product will look like

modifications changes to a design

oscillating swinging movement from side to side in an arc

output the result of a process – the end part to a system

pendulum swinging weight that moves in an oscillating motion

pinion toothed wheel that moves on a rack

piston cylinder with an attached rod which is driven back and forth by pressure

pivot point about which something, like a lever turns

property characteristic or quality of a material

prototype first version of a product, used for pre-production testing

reciprocating movement up and down or backwards and forwards

research finding out information about things

resistant materials hard materials that require force to cut or break them

rotary movement that turns around in a circular motion

scriber very fine pointed tool that traces lines by leaving a white mark on a surface

specification set of criteria that the final solution or finished product must achieve

sprocket wheel with teeth that fit into a chain

symmetrical exactly the same on both sides

target market type or group of people or companies that a product is aimed at

torque turning force

transmit move from one place to another

Resources

The following websites may be useful to look at when sourcing material and making the projects in this book:

www.automatomania.com/books.htm – information on books about automata

www.cabaret.co.uk – the Cabaret Mechanical Theatre website

www.designandtech.com – provides links to useful D & T websites, including school websites

www.designtechnology.org.uk – website created by the authors; dedicated to D & T education. It contains worksheets and project ideas.

www.flying-pig.co.uk – sells models to make

Disclaimer

All the Internet addresses (URLs) given in this book were valid at the time of going to press. However, due to the dynamic nature of the Internet, some addresses may have changed, or sites may have changed or ceased to exist since publication. While the author and Publishers regret any inconvenience this may cause readers, no responsibility for any such changes can accepted by either the author or the Publishers.

Index